FIRST CHAIR TRUMPET SOLOS

BRAHMS: *Academic Festival Overture* (EXCERPTS)

MENDELSSOHN: *Calm Sea and Prosperous Voyage Overture*

HANDEL: *Watermusic* (EXCERPTS)

BRUCKNER: *Symphony No. 3 in D minor* (EXCERPTS)

WAGNER: *Overture to Rienzi*

SUPPÈ: *Overture to the Light Cavalry* (EXCERPTS)

3806

COMPACT DISC PAGE AND BAND INFORMATION

MMO CD 3806
MMO Cass. 136

Music Minus One

FIRST CHAIR TRUMPET SOLOS

Complete Version: Band 1
Minus Trumpet: Band 14

Piccolo Trumpet
WATER MUSIC

B♭ Trumpet

HANDEL

Complete Version: Band 2
Minus Trumpet: Band 15

Complete Version: Band 3
Minus Trumpet: Band 16

14

Complete Version: Band 4
Minus Trumpet: Band 17

20

Both trumpets have been scored to facilitate performance.

SYMPHONY No.3

Complete Version: Band 5
Minus trumpet: Band 18

ANTON BRUCKNER

Complete Version: Band 6
Minus Trumpet: Band 19

Second excerpt

This is probably the first symphony ever written in which a trumpet renders the first theme accompanied by soft strings and woodwinds only.

Complete Version: Band 7
Minus Trumpet: Band 20

Bb Trumpet

ACADEMIC FESTIVAL OVERTURE

JOHANNES BRAHMS, Op. 80

Complete Version: Band 8
Minus Trumpet: Band 21

Bb Trumpet

LIGHT CAVALRY

FRANZ V. SUPPE

Complete Version: Band 10
Minus Trumpet: Band 23

Bb Trumpet

Complete Version: Band 11
Minus Trumpet: Band 24

CALM SEA AND PROSPEROUS VOYAGE

FELIX MENDELSSOHN BARTHOLDY, Op. 27

Complete Version: Band 12
Minus Trumpet Band 25

Bb Trumpet

RIENZI OVERTURE

RICHARD WAGNER

Bb Trumpet

14

Bb Trumpet

MUSIC MINUS ONE COMPACT DISC CATALOG

Music Minus One PIANO Compact Discs

__ MMO CD 3001 Beethoven Piano Concerto No. 1 in C, Opus 15
*MMO CD 3002 Beethoven Piano Concerto No. 2 in Bb, Opus 19
__ MMO CD 3003 Beethoven Piano Concerto No. 3 in Cm, Opus 37
*MMO CD 3004 Beethoven Piano Concerto No. 4 in G, Opus 58
*MMO CD 3005 Beethoven Piano Concerto No. 5 in Eb, Opus 73
__ MMO CD 3006 Grieg Piano Concerto in A minor, Opus 16
__ MMO CD 3007 Rachmaninoff Piano Concerto No. 2 in C minor
*MMO CD 3008 Schumann Piano Concerto in A minor, Opus 54
*MMO CD 3009 Brahms Piano Concerto No. 1 in D minor, Opus 15
__ MMO CD 3010 Chopin Piano Concerto No. 1 in Em, Opus 11
*MMO CD 3011 Mendelssohn Piano Concerto No. 1 in Gm, Opus 25
__ MMO CD 3012 W.A. Mozart Piano Concerto No. 9 in D, K.271
__ MMO CD 3013 W.A. Mozart Piano Concerto No. 12 in A, K.414
*MMO CD 3014 W.A. Mozart Piano Concerto No. 20 in Dm, K.466
__ MMO CD 3015 W.A. Mozart Piano Concerto No. 23 in A, K.488
__ MMO CD 3016 W.A. Mozart Piano Concerto No. 24 in Cm, K.491
*MMO CD 3017 W.A. Mozart Piano Concerto No. 26 in D, 'Coronation'
__ MMO CD 3018 W.A. Mozart Piano Concerto in G major, K.453
*MMO CD 3019 Liszt Piano Concerto No. 1/Weber Concertstucke
*MMO CD 3020 Liszt Piano Concerto No. 2/Hungarian Fantasia
__ MMO CD 3021 J.S. Bach Piano Concerto in Fm/J.C. Bach Concerto in Eb
__ MMO CD 3022 J.S. Bach Piano Concerto in D minor
__ MMO CD 3023 Haydn Piano Concerto in D major
*MMO CD 3024 Heart Of The Piano Concerto
*MMO CD 3025 Themes From The Great Piano Concerti
__ MMO CD 3026 Tschiakowsky Piano Concerto No. 1 in Bbm, Opus 23
*Available Spring 1995

Music Minus One VOCALIST Compact Discs

__ MMO CD 4001 Schubert Lieder for High Voice
__ MMO CD 4002 Schubert Lieder for Low Voice
__ MMO CD 4003 Schubert Lieder for High Voice   volume 2
__ MMO CD 4004 Schubert Lieder for Low Voice   volume 2
__ MMO CD 4005 Brahms Lieder for High Voice
__ MMO CD 4006 Brahms Lieder for Low Voice
__ MMO CD 4007 Everybody's Favorite Songs for High Voice
__ MMO CD 4008 Everybody's Favorite Songs for Low Voice
__ MMO CD 4009 Everybody's Favorite Songs for High Voice   volume 2
__ MMO CD 4010 Everybody's Favorite Songs for Low Voice   volume 2
__ MMO CD 4011 17th/18th Century Italian Songs High Voice
__ MMO CD 4012 17th/18th Century Italian Songs Low Voice
__ MMO CD 4013 17th/18th Century Italian Songs High Voice   volume 2
__ MMO CD 4014 17th/18th Century Italian Songs Low Voice   volume 2
__ MMO CD 4015 Famous Soprano Arias
__ MMO CD 4016 Famous Mezzo-Soprano Arias
__ MMO CD 4017 Famous Tenor Arias
__ MMO CD 4018 Famous Baritone Arias
__ MMO CD 4019 Famous Bass Arias
__ MMO CD 4020 Hugo Wolf Lieder for High Voice
__ MMO CD 4021 Hugo Wolf Lieder for Low Voice
__ MMO CD 4022 Richard Strauss Lieder for High Voice
__ MMO CD 4023 Richard Strauss Lieder for Low Voice
__ MMO CD 4024 Robert Schumann Lieder for High Voice
__ MMO CD 4025 Robert Schumann Lieder for Low Voice
__ MMO CD 4026 W.A. Mozart Arias For Soprano
__ MMO CD 4027 Verdi Arias For Soprano
__ MMO CD 4028 Italian Arias For Soprano
__ MMO CD 4029 French Arias For Soprano
__ MMO CD 4030 Soprano Oratorio Arias
__ MMO CD 4031 Alto Oratorio Arias
__ MMO CD 4032 Tenor Oratorio Arias
__ MMO CD 4033 Bass Oratorio Arias
John Wustman, Piano Accompanist

Music Minus One TRUMPET Compact Discs

__ MMO CD 3801 3 Trumpet Concerti   Handel/Telemann/Vivaldi
__ MMO CD 3802 Easy Solos, Student Edition, Beginning Level vol. 1
__ MMO CD 3803 Easy Solos, Student Edition, Beginning Level vol. 2
__ MMO CD 3804 Easy Jazz Duets with Rhythm Section, Beginning Level

Music Minus One TROMBONE Compact Discs

__ MMO CD 3901 Easy Solos, Student Editions, Beginning Level vol. 1
__ MMO CD 3902 Easy Solos, Student Editions, Beginning Level vol. 2
__ MMO CD 3903 Easy Jazz Duets, Student Editions, 1-3 years

Music Minus One ALTO SAX Compact Discs

__ MMO CD 4101 Easy Solos, Student Editions, Beginning Level vol. 1
__ MMO CD 4102 Easy Solos, Student Editions, Beginning Level vol. 2
__ MMO CD 4103 Easy Jazz Duets, Student Editions, 1-3 years

Music Minus One FRENCH HORN Compact Discs

__ MMO CD 3501 Mozart: Concerto No. 2, K.417; No. 3, K.447

Music Minus One GUITAR Compact Discs

__ MMO CD 3601 Boccherini: Guitar Quintet, No. 4 in D major
__ MMO CD 3602 Giuliani: Guitar Quintet, Opus 65
__ MMO CD 3603 Classic Guitar Duets Easy - Medium

Music Minus One CELLO Compact Discs

__ MMO CD 3701 Dvorak: Cello Concerto in B minor, Opus 104
__ MMO CD 3702 C.P.E. Bach: Cello Concerto in A minor
__ MMO CD 3703 Boccherini: Concerto in Bb Major; Bruch: Kol Nidrei

Music Minus One VIOLIN Compact Discs

__ MMO CD 3100 Bruch Violin Concerto in Gm
__ MMO CD 3101 Mendelssohn Violin Concerto in Em
__ MMO CD 3102 Tschaikovsky Violin Concerto in D, Opus 35
__ MMO CD 3103 J.S. Bach "Double" Concerto in Dm
__ MMO CD 3104 J.S. Bach Violin Concerti in Am/E
__ MMO CD 3105 J.S. Bach Brandenburg Concerti Nos. 4 and 5
__ MMO CD 3106 J.S. Bach Brandenburg No. 2/Triple Concerto
__ MMO CD 3107 J.S. Bach Concerto in Dm
*MMO CD 3108 Brahms Violin Concerto in D, Opus 77
*MMO CD 3109 Chausson Poeme/Schubert Rondo
__ MMO CD 3110 Lalo Symphonie Espagnole
__ MMO CD 3111 Mozart Concerto in D/Vivaldi Concerto in Am
__ MMO CD 3112 Mozart Violin Concerto in A, K.219
__ MMO CD 3113 Wieniawski Concerto in D/Sarasate Zigeunerweisen
__ MMO CD 3114 Viotti Concerto No. 22
__ MMO CD 3115 Beethoven Two Romances/''Spring'' Sonata
__ MMO CD 3116 St. Saëns Intro & Rondo Cap./Mozart Serenade & Adagio
__ MMO CD 3117 Beethoven Violin Concerto in D major, Opus 61
__ MMO CD 3118 The Concertmaster Solos from Symphonic Works
__ MMO CD 3119 Air On A G String Favorite Encores for Orchestra
__ MMO CD 3120 Concert Pieces For The Serious Violinist
__ MMO CD 3121 Eighteenth Century Violin Music
__ MMO CD 3122 Violin Favorites With Orchestra Vol. 1 (Easy)
__ MMO CD 3123 Violin Favorites With Orchestra Vol. 2 (Moderate)
__ MMO CD 3124 Violin Favorites With Orchestra Vol. 3 (Mod. Diff.)
__ MMO CD 3125 The Three B's: Bach/Beethoven/Brahms
__ MMO CD 3126 Vivaldi Concerti in Am, D, Am Opus 3 No. 6,9,8
__ MMO CD 3127 Vivaldi "The Four Seasons" 2 CD set $29.98 each
__ MMO CD 3128 Vivaldi "La Tempesta di Mare" Opus 8 No. 5
              Albinoni: Violin Concerto in A
__ MMO CD 3129 Vivaldi: Violin Concerto Opus 3 No. 12
*Spring 1995   Vivaldi Violin Concerto Opus 8, No. 6 ''Il Piacere''

Music Minus One FLUTE Compact Discs

__ MMO CD 3300 Mozart Concerto in D/Quantz Concerto in G
__ MMO CD 3301 Mozart Flute Concerto in G major
__ MMO CD 3302 J.S. Bach Suite No. 2 in Bm
__ MMO CD 3303 Boccherini/Vivaldi Concerti/Mozart Andante
__ MMO CD 3304 Haydn/Vivaldi/Frederick "The Great" Concerti
__ MMO CD 3305 Vivaldi/Telemann/Leclair Flute Concerti
__ MMO CD 3306 J.S. Bach Brandenburg No. 2/Haydn Concerto
__ MMO CD 3307 J.S. Bach Triple Concerto/Vivaldi Concerto No. 9
*MMO CD 3308 Mozart/Stamitz Flute Quartets
*MMO CD 3309 Haydn London Trios
*MMO CD 3310 J.S. Bach Brandenburg Concerti No. 4 and No. 5
*MMO CD 3311 W.A. Mozart Three Flute Quartets
*MMO CD 3312 Telemann Am Suite/Gluck 'Orpheus' Scene/Pergolesi Conc. in G
*MMO CD 3313 Flute Song Easy familiar Classics
__ MMO CD 3314 Vivaldi 3 Flute Concerti RV 427, 438, Opus 10 No. 5
__ MMO CD 3315 Vivaldi 3 Flute Concerti RV 440, Opus 10 No. 4, RV 429
__ MMO CD 3316 Easy Solos, Student Editions, Beginning Level vol. 1
__ MMO CD 3317 Easy Solos, Student Editions, Beginning Level vol. 2
__ MMO CD 3318 Easy Jazz Duets, Student Editions, 1-3 years
*Spring 1995

Music Minus One CLARINET Compact Discs

__ MMO CD 3201 Mozart Clarinet Concerto in A major
*MMO CD 3202 Weber Clarinet Concerto No. 1 in F minor, Op. 73
              Stamitz Clarinet Concerto No. 3 in Bb major
*MMO CD 3203 Spohr Clarinet Concerto No. 1 in C minor, Op. 26
*MMO CD 3204 Weber Clarinet Concertino, Opus 26
__ MMO CD 3205 First Chair Clarinet Solos Orchestral Excerpts
__ MMO CD 3206 The Art Of The Solo Clarinet Orchestral Excerpts
*MMO CD 3207 Mozart: Quintet for Clarinet and Strings in A, K.581
__ MMO CD 3208 Brahms: Sonatas Opus 120, Nos. 1 & 2
__ MMO CD 3209 Weber: Grand Duo Concertant - Wagner: Adagio
__ MMO CD 3210 Schumann Fantasy Pieces, Opus 73, Three Romances
__ MMO CD 3211 Easy Clarinet Solos, Student Editions 1-3 years
__ MMO CD 3212 Easy Clarinet Solos, Student Editions 1-3 years, vol. 2
__ MMO CD 3213 Easy Jazz Duets, Student Editions, 1-3 years
*Available Spring 1995

Music Minus One OBOE Compact Discs

__ MMO CD 3400 Albinoni Three Oboe Concerti Opus 7 No. 3, No. 6, Opus 9 No. 2
__ MMO CD 3401 3 Oboe Concerti: Handel, Telemann, Vivaldi
__ MMO CD 3402 Mozart/Stamitz Oboe Quartets in F major (K.370; Op.8 #3)

Music Minus One TENOR SAX Compact Discs

__ MMO CD 4201 Easy Tenor Sax Solos, Student Editions, 1-3 years
__ MMO CD 4202 Easy Tenor Sax Solos, Student Editions, 1-3 years
__ MMO CD 4103 Easy Jazz Duets with Rhythm Section, Beginning Level

Music Minus One BROADWAY Shows

__ MMO CD 1016 Les Mis/Phantom
__ MMO CD 1067 Guys And Dolls
__ MMO CD 1100 West Side Story (2 CD set)
__ MMO CD 1110 Cabaret
__ MMO CD 1173 Camelot
__ MMO CD 1174 My Fair Lady
__ MMO CD 1175 Oklahoma
__ MMO CD 1176 The Sound Of Music
__ MMO CD 1177 South Pacific
__ MMO CD 1178 The King And I
__ MMO CD 1179 Fiddler On The Roof
__ MMO CD 1180 Carousel
__ MMO CD 1181 Porgy And Bess
__ MMO CD 1183 The Music Man
__ MMO CD 1184 Showboat
__ MMO CD 1186 Annie Get Your Gun
__ MMO CD 1187 Hello Dolly
__ MMO CD 1189 Oliver (2 CD set)